SHARKS

By Gail Gibbons

Holiday House · New York

Special thanks to Robert Hueter and Kerry Kirschner
of Mote Marine Laboratory, Sarasota, Florida

Copyright © 1992 by Gail Gibbons
Printed in the United States of America

Library of Congress Cataloging-in-Publication Data
Gibbons, Gail.
Sharks / by Gail Gibbons.
p.   cm.
Summary: Describes shark behavior and different kinds of sharks.
ISBN 0-8234-0960-0
1. Sharks — Juvenile literature.   [1. Sharks.]   I. Title.
QL638.9.G383   1992   91-31524   CIP   AC
597′.31 — dc20
ISBN 0-8234-1068-4 (pbk.)

ISBN-13: 978-0-8234-0960-0 (hardcover)
ISBN-13: 978-0-8234-1068-2 (paperback)

ISBN-10: 0-8234-0960-0 (hardcover)
ISBN-10: 0-8234-1068-4 (paperback)

Sharks live in oceans. They are fish. There are about 350 different kinds of sharks.

There are small sharks, big sharks and . . .

huge sharks!

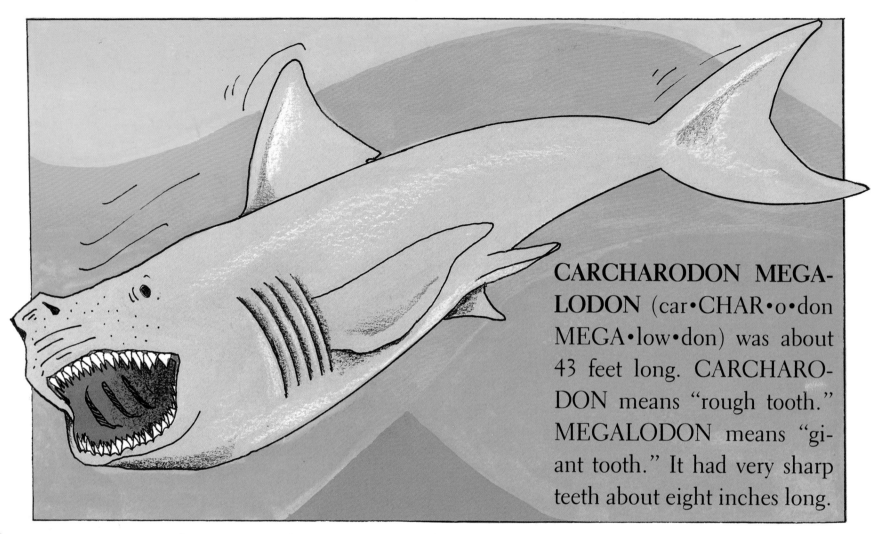

CARCHARODON MEGA-LODON (car•CHAR•o•don MEGA•low•don) was about 43 feet long. CARCHARODON means "rough tooth." MEGALODON means "giant tooth." It had very sharp teeth about eight inches long.

The first sharks lived more than 400 million years ago, 200 million years before dinosaurs walked the earth. Most of them were only about three feet long. Later, sharks grew to be bigger. Some were enormous. One of them was Carcharodon megalodon.

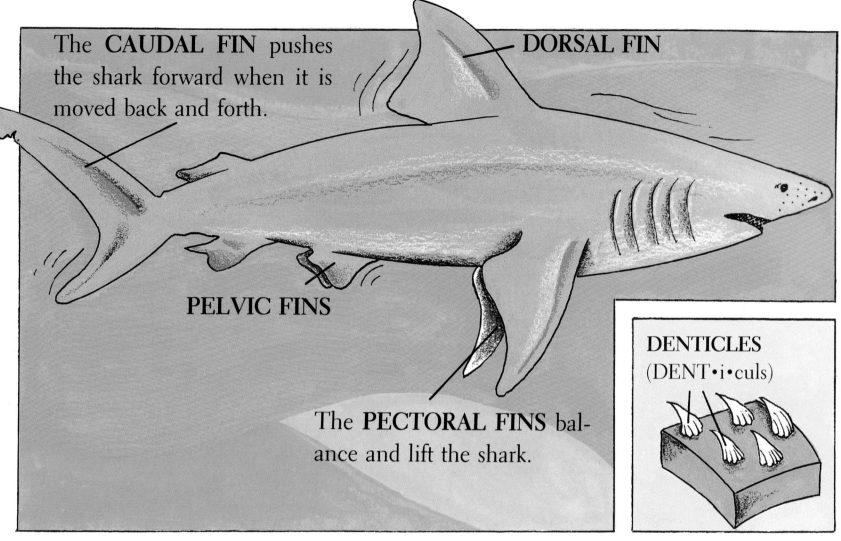

The **CAUDAL FIN** pushes the shark forward when it is moved back and forth.

DORSAL FIN

PELVIC FINS

The **PECTORAL FINS** balance and lift the shark.

DENTICLES
(DENT•i•culs)

Sharks are not like other fish. Fish have smooth scales. Sharks' bodies are covered with scales called denticles that have sharp little teeth in them. Most fish skeletons are made of bone. Shark skeletons are not made up of bone but a softer elastic material called cartilage.

Sharks have five, six or seven **GILL** openings on each side.

Other fish usually have one **GILL** opening on each side.

Sharks breathe by drawing water into their mouths as they swim. When the water passes the gills, it touches small blood vessels. These blood vessels take the oxygen from the water to keep the sharks alive. Unlike other fish, most sharks must keep moving to make the water flow over their gills.

LATERAL LINE ORGANS

Sharks have sharp senses that work together. They have inner ears. Their ears are tubes running under their skin to their skulls. They can hear distant sounds, even a heartbeat. On the sides of their bodies are small holes called lateral line organs. They are sensitive to movement in the water and can help guide the shark to what is moving.

AMPULLAE
(AM•pew•lee)

Sharks can use electricity to hunt, too. All living creatures in the water give off small electrical signals. Sharks have tiny holes in their faces called ampullae. They pick up the signals that guide the sharks in the right direction. Sharks also have a very good sense of smell. They can tell the direction a smell is coming from, sometimes a mile away.

Sharks' eyes are sensitive to light. They can see things under water where light is often dim.

Sharks don't use their teeth for chewing. They use their teeth to tear, bite and crush food. Most sharks have more than four rows of teeth. Their front teeth do all the work. When a shark loses a tooth, it will soon be replaced by a new one.

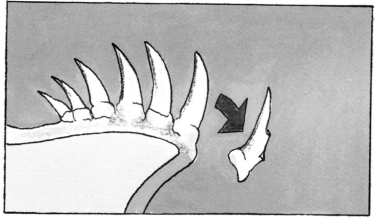

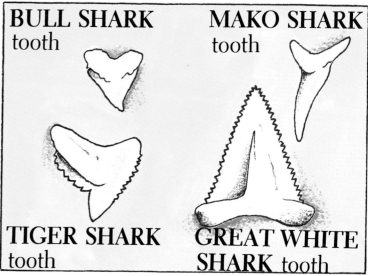

BULL SHARK tooth

MAKO SHARK tooth

TIGER SHARK tooth

GREAT WHITE SHARK tooth

New teeth move up from the second row. They replace worn out or missing teeth in the front row. The teeth in the third and fourth rows move forward, too. Different sharks have teeth that are different sizes and shapes.

EGG

Shark babies are born two ways. Some sharks lay tough, thorny cased eggs on or near the bottom of the ocean. It takes a few weeks before the baby sharks chew their way out of the egg cases and swim away.

Other sharks develop from eggs inside the mother's body. Usually it takes about a year before these babies are born alive. Shark babies can care for themselves from the minute they are born. They are called pups.

Most sharks are not dangerous. Of the 350 kinds of sharks, only about 30 species have been known to attack people. This rarely happens. When it does, it usually is because the shark has mistaken the movement of a person for the movement of a fish or something else it is hunting.

The smallest shark is the **DWARF SHARK.** It is only six inches long.

Sharks are different shapes and sizes.

BULL SHARKS are about ten feet long. They are fierce and aggressive. They've been known to attack people who are swimming. Bull sharks are the only kind of shark that can live in fresh water. On rare occasions they are spotted swimming in rivers.

BLUE SHARKS usually live in deep waters. They migrate thousands of miles to have their babies and search for new food.

MAKO SHARKS can be up to 11 feet long and can swim as fast as 43 miles an hour! They can be dangerous.

TIGER SHARKS can grow up to 17 feet long. They are often found in shallow water. Tiger sharks eat fish, sea-birds, crabs, turtles and even smaller sharks. They are one of the most dangerous sharks.

The **THRESHER SHARK** can be up to 20 feet long. It has a very long, powerful tail. It eats small fish and usually doesn't bother people.

NURSE SHARKS often hide in underwater caves and reefs for long periods of time. They have strong, blunt teeth. They eat fish, shrimp, lobster, sea urchins and crabs.

HAMMERHEAD SHARKS can be almost 20 feet long and are strange looking. Their heads are flat and shaped like a double-headed hammer. They eat fish, squid, crabs and stingrays. Hammerhead sharks live in shallow, warm waters and have been known to attack people.

GREAT WHITE SHARKS are famous for being the most dangerous and fiercest members of the shark family. They will eat large fish, other sharks and even whales.

It has very strong jaws and hundreds of teeth, sometimes three inches long. Each tooth has a sharp jagged edge like a saw blade.

The **BASKING SHARK** is very large and can grow to be about 35 feet long. It is slow moving and generally harmless. It eats small animals and plant life called plankton.

The **BASKING SHARK** likes to swim near the surface of the water, sometimes in large groups.

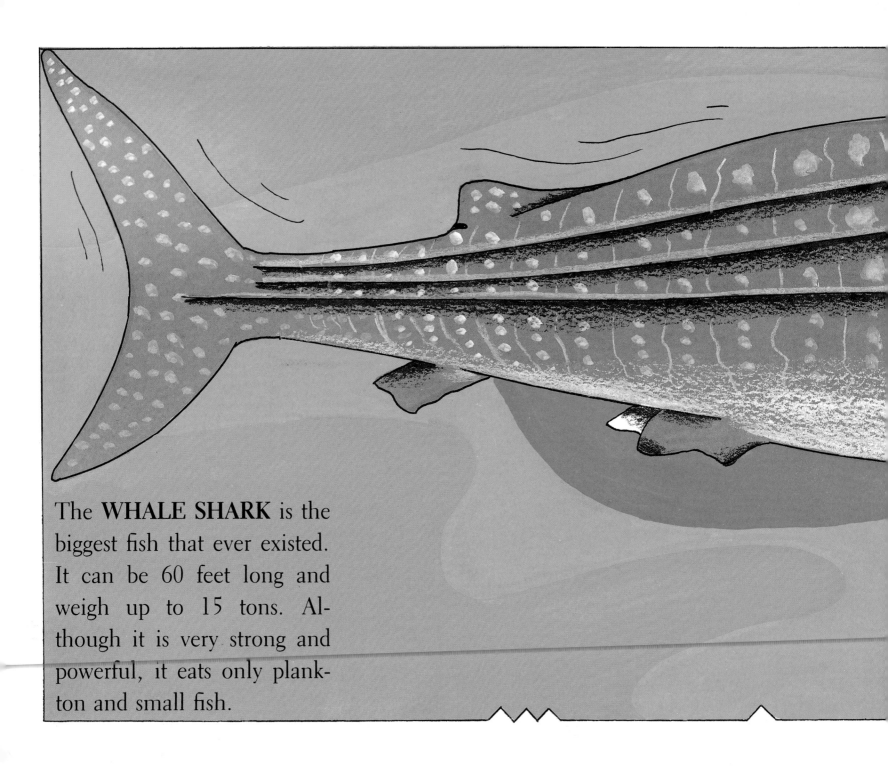

The **WHALE SHARK** is the biggest fish that ever existed. It can be 60 feet long and weigh up to 15 tons. Although it is very strong and powerful, it eats only plankton and small fish.

The **WHALE SHARK** never attacks people or even large fish. It swims slowly and lazily, usually just below the surface of the water.

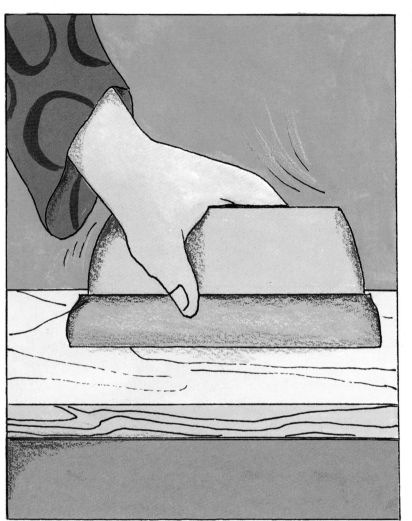

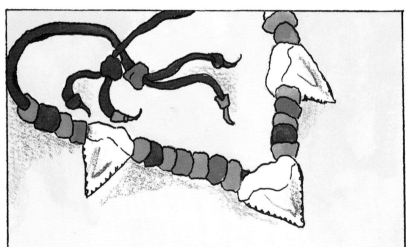

For many years sharks have been fished and hunted by people. Before sandpaper was invented, people used shark skin to smooth and polish wood. Indians used sharp, hard shark teeth for arrowheads. Others used shark teeth for jewelry.

Today, in some places, shark skin is used to make shoes, purses and belts. Also, shark meat is used for food. There is sport fishing, too. Some species have been fished and hunted to the point where there is concern about their survival.

Sharks play an important role, like all other ocean life. It is good to protect these mysterious and marvelous creatures and the sea in which they live.

Scientists and people can learn a lot from studying sharks.
To know about sharks is to admire and respect them.

...SHARKS...SHARKS...SHARKS...

The whale shark lays the world's biggest egg. It is about 12 inches long!

Scientists have learned that sharks don't get cancer. Studying sharks might help in the fight against cancer.

The whale shark has skin thicker than any other creature. It is up to 8 inches thick.

A person is more likely to be killed by lightning or a bee sting than by a shark.

IMPORTANT . . .

If you see a shark when you are swimming . . .

Slowly swim away from the shark toward the shore or boat.

The chances are the shark isn't interested in you and will swim away.

Remain calm. Don't shout or splash.

Remember, you are in the shark's world. Don't swim toward the shark.

If you are around other people when you reach the shore or boat, tell someone in authority what you saw so other swimmers can be notified.